She Is Strong

Empowering Women to Rise

Eileen Hunter Wolf

MANIFOLD GRACE
Publishing House LLC

Cover graphics: Creativelogoart
Photog-cover design: Karlton Putnam

ISBN: 978-1-937400-53-8

Printed in the United States of America

Manifold Grace Publishing House, LLC
Southfield, Michigan 48033
www.manifoldgracepublishinghouse.com

God Bless you!

Ellen H. White

Dedication

I dedicate this book to my cherished sister, Yvette, and to all those who are still battling! Even in the struggle, may you capture all that God sees in you. Sister, daughter, friend, you are worth fighting for.

Acknowledgment

To my Lord and Savior Jesus Christ, you have prepared good things in advance, I pray that all I do is for your glory.

To *Mamá*, your courage and love has shaped me, I can look at you and live my best, with no excuses.

To *my godly mentor*, Mother Hunter, I have never seen a woman walk so close with God.

To *my strong sisters*, Licette, Cecilia, Enorita, Darlene, Donna, Josie, Judy, Shirley, Faye, Elsie, Julia, and Christine thank you for being women of great character.

To *my little leaders*, Lauren, Olivia, Trinity, Dalicia, and Jessica, may you passionately live out God's dream for your life.

To *my son*, Israel, my heart is filled with love for you, always pursue God's best!

To *my Lb*, you have made room for every potential gift in me and have supported all God has called me to become. Thank you for the way you love me.

Table of Contents

Contents

Foreword

It is always a privilege and an honor to publish a family member; but in the case of Eileen Hunter Wolf, it is magnified times ten! She is such a beautiful woman, and at the risk of sounding cliché, inside and out. I met her when my brother, Roosevelt Hunter, brought her home. There was an excitement in his voice as he contemplated whether or not to tell me he thought she was the one. Well, you don't get to be the big sister of four brothers without knowing these things. I could tell right away how special she would be.

We met and my instincts were right on. She instantly became a member of the family, even before they married and after she gave us a beautiful niece and nephew, it was a lock! It is my pleasure to say these things about Eileen, but that's not what I need to share with you. I watched her become a single mother as she closed the door on the woman married to my brother, the partner and support in his evangelistic ministry and founder of her own women's ministry. And it took a while for new doors to open to her – I believe it is called the grieving period.

During that time, she tried to determine what she should be doing. She'd had a busy life with Roosevelt, often traveling all over the world to minister alongside him, this changed once she had children and it changed even more dramatically once he was gone. Eileen focused on being the world's best mom, she is tenacious on most days. But she kept submitting her life to God, she kept seeking God for direction. After all, her previous dreams were tied to a reality that no longer existed. She slowly began to share her testimony how God worked things out; how He healed her broken heart and how she found purpose and fulfillment in telling others they could surely overcome.

"God is so faithful!" she would minister. "You have to believe; your faith has to stand on the word of God because God will do what His word says!"

Before long, Eileen Hunter was preaching in Malawi, Africa; one of the last places Roosevelt preached. Before long, people were reaching out to Eileen because her message of hope, faith, mercy and grace hit a spot in their lives. Before long Eileen Hunter married Larry Wolf and now had four 'treasures' as she says. Larry is a wonderful, supportive husband and father and my new brother. I won't tell you how long 'long' is because, as Eileen would say, "God is good even when bad things happen" or "God has the ability to bring grace and transformation in His perfect time frame, not yours".

Eileen Hunter Wolf has written a love letter to women; a word of encouragement that cannot fail. She shares her testimony; she shares the word of God; inviting you to hang on to every word. You're going to love this workbook, because when you absorb the principles, you will see for yourself – *She Is Strong!*

Darlene Carol Dickson
CEO, Manifold Grace Publishing House, LLC
May 5, 2019

Introduction: Stronger Than the Struggle

There are women all around us who are remarkably strong, not because of their physical strength but because they possess the ability to rise above the opposition. What causes so many of us to get through circumstances and others to give up on the journey? The power to prevail is available to all of us, but is seldom seen when we are in the heat of the battle; just trying to keep it all together. There are many legitimate excuses that keep us stuck in the middle of our mess; with no chance of hope. Then there are those among us, women who decide in their heart to know the one who can turn weakness into strength. These are women who choose to climb by strategically leveraging their inability for something greater, the need for a savior.

For the Christ follower, the source of our strength is not found in our unmatched skill or our positive determination. There is a scripture that states, *"I can do all things through Christ who gives me strength"* (Phil. 4:13). Now let's be clear, it would be absolutely insane for me to think I have the strength to do anything I want to do, anytime I want to do it. Our personal strengths ultimately allow us to skillfully function in areas that we have dedicated intentional practice time to. The law of gravity, inertia, and common sense reminds us of our boundaries. Even if I desired to fly, I cannot jump into the sky or become a ready-made pilot. The only way I am flying is if I purchase a ticket for a seat on an aircraft. I humbly recognize that I am subject to governing principles. God is sovereign, but I am not. So then, what was Paul expressing when he wrote this to the first western church in the city of Philippi?

Strength is accessible to us through the power of Christ. We are able to do everything God has created and ordained for us to creatively accomplish, through following Him. God has a beautiful story that is unfolding with each day that you live. He has the ability to accomplish His great plans for you. We never have to worry about not having what it takes, because we don't, He does. In order to fulfill our purpose and finish strong, we must walk in the path that allows us to trust in Christ. In a self-sufficient world, we can certainly take the approach to choose our way of doing things, but if we live by that low standard, it will leave us wanting. Many of us choose not to tap into the authority we have in Christ because it is painful to deny our flesh and submit to Him.

My seasoned friend, who is a former marine says, "Pain is weakness leaving your body, so keep on fighting". What a way to look at pain. The reality is, there are many times our weakness is glaring back at us with great disappointment. Real weakness is, never allowing or making room for God's strength to be our ultimate source. Without Him we will live a tragically painful life, chasing after things and not having acquired lasting peace. Paul talked about boasting in his weakness, because once he found Christ, he knew life would ultimately be worth living. When we depend on our power, we will come up short, and wonder if there is more to the life we are meant to live.

You and I are called to go the distance. Paul wrote this to the Philippians who were facing persecution for being Christ followers. The only way the first century church would successfully survive was to endure hardship. In each of our lives, there are battle fronts that we must engage. Think of this book as a tool you can use to help you grow stronger. At the end of each chapter you will be introduced to strength training skills. As we take a closer look into the narrative, you can extract each woman's struggle and see how her inspiring transformation took place. As you reflect on each of these women, you will find practical applications for today. The workbook portion is designed to motivate you to live out what you just learned. I encourage you do the work as personal devotion between you and God, or to do this in a small group setting with friends. Invite God to be a personal coach in the moments where life becomes challenging. We will take time to evaluate who we are, what must be protected, how to cope with suffering, and lastly how to keep your strength. You can go the distance because the Christ in you has the power to go the distance. We wrestle with our worth and value, depression and loss. Warriors continue to win battles because, with Christ we are stronger than the struggle.

Let's face it, what a relief to know you're not the only one in life in need of strength. The struggles we face are a natural part of the journey, therefore our weakness does not have to be the final experience in our story. When we encounter tough times, we should learn to get up, shake things off, evaluate our experience, and keep on going. Getting where we need to be is not quite that simple, so how do we rise above the struggle? Learning from the stories of other women around us will encourage us. Transforming our disappointments into notable victories is the personal goal. Some of history's leading ladies were far from flawless, but they are recognized and remembered because of their wisdom, courage, and strength. As we take a closer look at the lives and stories we read, we can come away confidently knowing that we don't have to be perfect to be powerful. What allowed these women to rise above the setbacks is what will inspire us to live as healthy, Christian women in our generation.

Becoming free to enjoy the life God has called you to is possible even while you are walking through a process. There is an impending battle, set in place to keep you from accomplishing God's best. Although there is an invisible enemy that would love to wrestle you down with fear and worry, you are God's warrior. I invite you to live an armed and dangerous life. We can get through the stumbling blocks of stress, rejection, and guilt so that you can fully embrace grace, freedom, and joy. You will come away from these pages empowered by the practical truth that these life lessons will bring. It will inspire and equip you as you continue to serve God and the world around you. Give yourself permission to get strong, and live with a resolve that you are built to be stronger than the struggle you are in.

Growing Stronger,

Eileen

Life Lesson 1

Battle with Identity ~ Becoming

"When one has fully entered the realm of love, the world, no matter how imperfect – becomes rich and beautiful, it consists solely on opportunities to love." - Søren Kierkegaard

My pregnant mom was carrying her fourth child when she heard a gripping news report about a forgotten baby, abandoned in a hotel room. A concerned doctor, staying across the hallway, responded to the hollering and urgently investigated the trouble. The deserted baby girl was retrieved, but not fit to be returned to the neglectful parents or family. The compassionate doctor and his wife walked through the necessary process of adopting her and calling her by her new name, Eileen. This family reclaimed her as one of their own and gave her the privilege of becoming a daughter. She now belonged to them and this would give her the ability to live a strong and healthy life. Several months later when I was born, my mother decided to call me by that same name. That news story reminded her of how love gave this innocent little child an opportunity to triumph against the odds.

From inception, love has the power to redeem us and redefine who we truthfully are. Eve, the first created woman, is both cherished and valued by her Creator. She is fashioned in love and set apart for God's glory. Long before she is given the responsibility to lead others, she is given the security of knowing that she has a unique place in God's heart. Her identity is first established because she belonged to a perfect Heavenly Father who has never rejected her as His daughter. Like Eve, you are loved and accepted because you belong. Your belonging to God, is the launching pad that springs forth your becoming.

We belong to God and before you took your first breath, He knew the real you. God knows who you are and you bring great joy to your Heavenly Father way before you decide to achieve purpose. God feels this way about each of you, "*You saw who you created me to be before I became me! Before I'd ever seen the light of day, the number of days you planned for me were already recorded in your book. Every single moment you are thinking of me! How precious and wonderful to consider that you cherish me constantly in your every thought! O God, your desires toward me are more than the grains of sand on every shore! When I awake each morning, you're still with me.*" Psalm 139:16-18 (TPT)

God creates each human being with an innate desire to be known and to be connected. We can contribute from who we are. Eve and her husband, Adam, were created into God's family, then they were set in a garden called Eden to manage and steward the earth through each of their God given strengths. We are also created with dignity and honor, which is the reason our hearts long to worship and bring honor. In its proper place, worship belongs solely to the Creator, but our hearts will crave the chance to give attention or allegiance to something created if awe is not given to God. When we experience who God is, we will attribute worth and glory to Him and in turn, He allows us to also live honorable lives. We have been fashioned first to be close to God, to honor Him, and also to reflect Him in our service to others.

The heart of the Father is best seen through the life of Jesus Christ, the anointed son of God. Jesus is the exact reflection of the father's heart on the earth. His mission was to serve and His fame was that He was a friend of sinners. While we were yet separated from God's holiness, because of our sin, the love of Jesus sacrificially made a way for us to be reconciled through the cross. Your shortcomings do not have the power to override God's ability to redeem who you are meant to become. No matter how far our sin happens to take us, we can call out to Him as His children and turn in His direction. His love will claim you, not as orphans, but as children who are unconditionally loved. Just when you think you are fighting on your own, you can rest assured that you have not been abandoned. Christ made it possible to access God's presence anytime we need to. As a child of God, you have someone that loves you and cares about the tiny details of your life. God never chooses to watch over you with indifference, but He longs to act, for your best interest and to put you in a place that you are provided for; by His grace.

The devil tried to convince Eve that she should do life without the involvement of God. He opposes everything God says about who you really are. Eve was convinced that she could be self-reliant and not have to turn to her Heavenly Father for her needs. Our sinful nature draws a circle around us, and makes you and I the center of our strongest desires, and the ultimate answer to our final decision. Sin blinds you to who you are and lies to you about your ability to overcome. Your problem is never bigger than God. Before you come to realize it, your sin forces God out and makes you the focus. *"The fool says in his heart that there is no God"* (Psalm 14:1). It is foolish to live independently from a loving creator who wants to engage in our everyday affairs. Your biggest problem is that you are no longer looking for God to be a part of the small details of your life and involve Him only when necessary. Your heart will never be satisfied until you surrender your self-reliance and allow God to rescue you from pride.

Unfortunately, it is natural to struggle and lose your identity if you choose to live independently from the one who made you. Without Him, you will not know who you are or who you are meant to become. Our eyes and heart must shift to who God really is in order for you to understand the truth of who you are. He is capable and willing to work things out because He is motivated by love for you. His faithful care for us is there to guide us, direct us, and walk with us as we invite Him to take the lead.

Our identity is not based on the materials we own, or the tasks that we do. Eve was fixed on what she could not have and got caught in the comparison trap. Identity is rooted in who you know God is, in relationship to you. His love is strong enough to reach you, even when life doesn't go according to your plan. Knowing that kind of redeeming love allows you to receive His provision and protection as His child, even if you are wounded or weak.

Hurtful names have a way of robbing you of your true identity. I can recall getting through the zany middle school years and then through the uncertainties of high school. I was called several names, some of them were cute and funny and others were less desirable. With God's wisdom, I simply decided that although people assign labels, not all of them are worth keeping. How we see ourselves can keep us from experiencing the love God longs to individually provide for you. The illusion of a better life without God will leave you confused, and searching for an alternate plan; other than your personal best. You have been designed for a profound life that is customized only for you. You will never become who He has called you to be apart from believing and accepting God's truth.

What was meant to destroy Eve and her family would shape her as a worshipper and a warrior; when she turned back to Him. Through grace, our greatest weapon is to trust, invite God's presence to be close, worship Him for who He is, and then believe that He will get involved and direct your next step. We have the ability to reclaim who we are in Christ. We have the power to become, because of who God is and what he did for us. It's just like that news report about the abandoned infant crying in the hotel room, she was experiencing rejection until a compassionate doctor rescued her and became her adopted father. God rescues us and gives us the opportunity to live strong healthy lives that are rooted in His redeeming love. We can get up when we mess up, come to God and ask Him to guide each moment because His love is stronger than our deficit. You can triumph against the odds because you mean the world to Him.

It is amazing to think that Eve's story would continue long after her, and that her legacy would bring forth the promised Messiah, Jesus Christ. She became the one God used to eventually bring forth amazing grace in the aftermath of all of our sin. You don't have to settle with living separated in your sin, or living with regret - you belong to God. Let go of your self-sufficiency and humbly accept God's help. Remind yourself that His strength will make the difference for your inadequacy. His grace will pick you up from your messy situation and allow you to walk with confidence as children who are dearly loved and provided for. Never forget that in the middle of your struggle you have not lost everything; because He is with you. He loved you first, and He will move heaven and earth to let you know He is for you.

"In all these things we are more than conquerors through him who loved us. For I am sure that neither death nor life, nor angels nor rulers, nor things present nor things to come, nor powers, nor height nor depth, nor anything else in all creation, will be able to separate us from the love of God in Christ Jesus our Lord." (Romans 8:37-39 ESV)

You are loved, valued, redeemed, and therefore you can become loving, strong, and powerful. You are the reflection of a perfect God, loving imperfect people. All that He says we are - is true. God sees you in light of His son Jesus, who did not die to leave you powerless or weak. He desires to show His strength through you, because you live dependent on His love to guide you. Even in your weakness, you are able to successfully accomplish what you have been created for, because it is God's love that empowers you to be all you are meant to become.

There is an argument that states, "truth is relative" which means if you believe or experience something to be true, then it simply is. In moments like this, I want to reply, "Is that your opinion or is that absolutely true?" Truth has stood the test of time and is not subject to how I feel or what I think. If your personal truth, is not absolute truth, then how can it stand? Your life will be unstable and shifting. The real struggle comes when we repeatedly surrender to a lie, rather than remain held together by the declaration from heaven over ourselves and our future. If we can recall what happens to the female warrior Eve, we understand this was the introduction to her downfall.

She sought after the forbidden knowledge from the tree of good and evil, and was willing to step outside of God's blessing to go after her desires. Unprotected, she steps out and finds herself wounded from the fight. It is a deadly trap. She thought she was missing out, but what she didn't realize was the hefty price she would pay for her poor decision. She focused on her lack, but the truth revealed that she already had what she needed. These fatal attractions set us up for unnecessary failure because it exposes our weakness. We never intend for the battle to turn for the worst, but all of a sudden, the door leads you to a place where we are bleeding and hurting from the terrible fall.

Lies have the power to slay you. Your identity seems to remind you that you don't have a desirable life, but that is not the truth of who you are. As you look at your reflection, you must declare your emancipation from these lies. God's love is always stronger than your fall. He wants to protect and provide for you, but first you must come to Him with a humble heart. You don't ever have to hide from the one who loves us, forgives us, and redeems us. If you have opened the door to temptation and walked into a trap called sin, then open another door called repentance. It will provide you with strength for your mistakes. He will give you the grace to stand strong again by the blood of Christ that reconciles you. His redeeming love is the strongest power there is.

He will lift you up and draw you close, even when guilt has let you down and dropped you low. He is the way out of destruction, because He rebuilds and restores you. This is the absolute truth about your Heavenly Father. God so loves you that He willingly reconciles us to Himself. When you are in the middle of your mess, never forget that. Be confident of this, that you come from greatness and His unconditional love wants to be amplified in your heart, no matter how far you have fallen. You are becoming. You are a warrior who can take a hit in the battle, who is determined to stay under His command. You may stumble, but you remain strong.

Strategic Battle Plans:

- Fight for what is true
- Close the door to temptation, or else it will make room for sin

- Open the door to repentance
- Let love in, by drawing close to God
- Humble yourself and receive forgiveness
- Allow grace to make you gracious to others

Declarations:

"Standing on the truth is stronger than trusting in a lie. "

"God's love is stronger than my fall. "

God's redeeming love is stronger than your struggle. Have you lived removed, or lived with regret? Like Eve, reclaim His love and allow it to make a difference in who you are.

1. Eve is cherished by God and individually created for His presence and honor. She has a special place in His heart and belongs to God's family. Adam and Eve reflect God's image and are blessed to bring their leadership into the earth. They are equal in essence, yet different in role. They are each empowered to give from their individual strengths.

2. The enemy looks for an opportune time to ultimately get her to believe a lie that she should live independent from God. Through satan, he strategically paints images before her placing toxic thoughts in her heart. She must face her sinful decision, and pays the consequence that affect her and others.

3. God promises that the Messiah would come and crush the evil one. We have lasting hope that comes with

believing that Jesus will come and rescue all who believe in Him. God loves us too much to leave us separated from Him. He makes a way through Jesus to restore us back to relationship.

Scripture References: How did Eve overcome this struggle? (found in the book of Genesis) How does her story help me in the battle for my identity?

_____

_____

_____

_____

_____

_____

_____

_____

_____

_____

_____

_____

Observations: Your True Identity

- As a woman you are:
    - → loved and valued by God
    - → created to reflect God's image on the earth
- As a worshipper:
    - → You are made for God's glory, not for your own fame
    - → God's presence is made known in your praise
- As a warrior:
    - → God's love will fight for you
    - → You have the ability to triumph against the odds

Table Talk:

1. What is the Lord speaking to you about identity?
2. Do you ever get caught in the comparison trap? In what ways?
3. Is there an area where the enemy is tempting you?
4. Name two areas that God has called you to contribute or help?
5. You are a warrior equipped for battle. Talk about how God can help you overcome a struggle you are facing in this season.
6. Name a cause that keeps you passionate?
7. How do you see God's grace at work in your life?
8. Share a blessing that causes you to worship God.

Application:

How did God respond to Eve's mistakes? How will He respond to your mistakes?

_____

_____

_____

_____

Home Project:

God made you, write a few adjectives that describe you:

_____

_____

_____

_____

Measure the lies against the truth of God's Word, write one promise from His word:

_____

_____

_____

Quality Time – Growing Stronger

Day 1: Read Psalm 139:1-6, 13-18
Write a few ways you see God's wonder in your life.

_____

_____

_____

_____

Day 2: Read Jeremiah 5:5-9
Write a few areas that you plan to walk in obedience to God

_____

_____

_____

_____

Day 3: Read James 1:19-25
God's Word reflects the true you. What lie do you need to stop believing?

_____

_____

_____

_____

Day 4: Read Numbers 6:24-26

Speak God's blessing over yourself, then write down the name of someone you should speak to, then encourage them this week.

_____

_____

_____

_____

Day 5: Read Romans 6:11-14

How has God's grace helped you to live differently?

_____

_____

_____

_____

Life Lesson 2

Battle with Grief and Loss ~ Beautifully Broken

"All the adversity I've had in my life, all my troubles and obstacles have strengthened me." - Walt Disney

Seattle, Washington is home for me and a few million other people. In this popular city, we go through many grey days. From October through June, you must prepare for scattered showers, partial sun, and cloudy skies in the forecast. People can let that get them down, but for so many of us, we decide to just grab a sweatshirt and deal with it. What's not to enjoy when you take in the true beauty of this wonderful city? We delight in the moderate temperatures, lush evergreens, and the breathtaking landscape. We visit our nearest coffee roaster and take time to express who we are through a variety of venues. It's one of the top places to live, with so much to offer, but if you look closely you will also find some residents grumbling about the conditions. Embracing where you are, even when life seems heavy, takes a maturity that's rooted in our struggles. Happiness can be as fluctuating as each circumstance we encounter. Keep this as a simple reminder, you're never going to stop the rain by complaining (that song just popped into my head).

Why should we ever feel good about loss? Grief is unpleasant, and without a doubt the one left grieving would agree. Getting through the valley requires lots of determination. A loss is both personal and painful and no matter what type of sorrow you face, it is never easy. But as much as it is not welcomed, it is unavoidable, so we might as well find a way to work through it. There are plenty of reasons people, and situations, change and I can never rationalize that walking through loss will initially make me wiser or stronger. To tell you the truth, my survival skills usually consist of lots of prayers and deep, heavy breathing.

I am no stranger to the dark, as I survived the unexpected change that would come into my world through the loss of my spouse. Looking back, I was frozen in my inability to think rationally, and paralyzed in my steps to move forward. I thought that my can-do attitude would help, but reluctantly it did not, and that was even more shocking for me. I didn't know how to ask for, or receive help. I could hear my heart pound as I considered my totally transformed life. The overwhelming thought was, I was not sure how much of me was ready to keep on living.

The truth about grief and loss, is that staying away from it won't make it disappear. We must first accept that it has happened and as hopeless as we may feel, it is not the end of us. Healing will never come if hope is not welcomed into your broken heart. When it's dark, where will you turn for comfort in the middle of your pain? When I lost my husband, Roosevelt, to a battle with cancer, I wasn't quite sure if my soul would ever recover. As a single mom to the littlest wonders in my life, I had to accept my new reality. I found myself drowning in a pool of disappointment, but I couldn't remain that way and stay healthy.

This sad season you are in, can also be a continuation of God's handiwork. You are a display of priceless art crafted by the Creator's hand. He can hold you together with comfort and love and display an extraordinary story behind all of the pieces even the broken ones. People may say that time heals all wounds, but it is not true. We must find comfort in the healing words of life, and for me, that is more than likely found in God's Word. *"They will rebuild the ancient ruins and restore the places devastated; they will renew the ruined cities that have been devastated for generations"* (Isaiah 61:4). I had to choose life, even when death was pressing in and weighing me down. Fear wanted to own me, but I had to redirect it out of my life. My hope in Christ reminded me that yes, my life had changed, but my pain was not permanent. My dreams were lost, my heart shattered, and yet God had the ingenuity to do something with all the fragmented pieces that were surrounding me. He could do it when I couldn't see what I could still become. He rebuilds and creates an exceptional mosaic with our brokenness.

There are a lot of layers to grief, one of them is love. We must come to realize that love is what causes us to grieve. Buried beneath the layers of sorrow, we discover that our sadness is connected to the joy of having experienced a deep and meaningful relationship with someone we cherish. This is sincerely true about my late husband, Roosevelt. There is no getting over the scar, but there is getting through the struggle, knowing that I am better for having loved someone so precious. I cannot control the circumstance that occurred, and I cannot undo what has been done. I can, however, live with the hope that my sadness is temporary.

Don't live life always trying to dodge the rain, because you will still be drenched in the end. Instead, let the water fall and when it's done look for the rainbow. There does come a colorful glimpse of beauty arching through the sky to remind all of those who look upon it. You have been given a priceless gift that can bring splendor to others when life showers down on them. The color of rain is seen in your resilient strength to live with an eternal hope that transcends the human heart (Ecclesiastes 3:11).

How would Naomi fill the emptiness that held her captive to anger and bitterness? Drowning in her affliction, she struggles to find strength as she walked through loss (Ruth 1:1-5). How do we prepare for the unexpected changes along the journey? Naomi's bitterness could have been the end of her, but somehow, she pulls through in the face of adversity. On a quest to discover a new adventure, she leaves her homeland and travels out with her husband and two boys to relocate to a new culture and city in Moab. It is here that her boys marry two Moabite women, Orpha and Ruth. It is also here that Naomi's husband, Elimelek, dies. She believes for the best, but sadly her personal dreams are visited by yet another tragedy as she walks through the death of her two sons. The unimaginable had come, and she had nothing left to offer, not even the hope of having another son. Encouraging her grieving daughters-in-law to depart and remarry, Ruth chooses to remain with Naomi and travel back to Bethlehem in Judah. Ruth and Naomi continue to help and serve each other as they walk through their sorrow. We must humbly come to God and get honest about our heavy heart and our need for help, God generously pours out good things to all who graciously receive him (Psalm 84:11).

God invites us to trust Him even when we feel hurt and stay distant. Naomi would soon find out that God is good, even when situations are bad. He is present to help in our trouble (Psalm 46:1). He wants to be our source of strength in the transition of each season we encounter. Leaving negativity behind, Naomi embraced the grace to get through it. He fills their lives with the great joy of a grandson and He restores hope and strength. Jesus promises to lead us to the other side of despair as the author of life continues to write our remarkable story.

I discovered that so many people could identify with what I walked through even if their loss was not a loved one. As a single parent for many years, I traveled and shared my personal story of finding hope in my darkest hour. People survived tragedy through betrayal, miscarriage, and bank-ruptcy and some people were grappling with their own health issues. Their sudden change felt impossible and life became overwhelming. I got on the plane and told my story in a variety of cities and churches, but I also picked up the phone and listened to so many stories of those who were going through hardship. The one story that would change my life forever, was from a longtime friend Larry Wolf. My late husband, Roosevelt, introduced me to him and his wife Robin back in the day. Listening to his reality, after losing his wife of 24 years was difficult. He believed God as he held his family together as a single dad.

What are the necessary steps that we can take as we walk through grief or loss of any kind? We can understand that we are in a difficult transition which means we are not there yet, but getting stronger. It is a temporary season, so be prepared to navigate through unpredictable moments. Spend time praying and listening. Ask God for wisdom, grace, and help on the road to where you need to go. When it's clear, determine the direction you should find necessary. For Naomi, it was allowing Ruth to go with her during a time she felt depressed and lonely. For me, it was receiving specific care from my church community and allowing them to help me with my practical needs.

Lastly, we must embrace the change. We must give ourselves permission to grieve and get honest with our new reality. We may not know what to choose or how to get there. In these tough times do not allow everything to have equal weight. Before we make the decision to figure out life, let's first decide it is ok to hurt before we heal. Although it feels like you have been forced to let go of a loved one, you can still cherish the love that has the power to help you carry on. Choose to let love in by letting others walk with you. It is an indicator that you are good, even in the grief. Decide to open your heart to comfort and heal. You will find that life does go on and we do not have to fear the change that takes place.

My Story: The Wolf (Larry) did eventually catch The Hunter (that's me). My friend Larry, was healing and so were his beloved daughters. It was not much longer before we both discovered that God was weaving our stories together. He asked me to marry him and together raise all our treasures. We then moved to the Pacific Northwest. I would have never guessed God would see fit to blend our family and make us one. Now, I have double for my trouble with two more remarkable children and an outstanding husband. I never would have thought, that as dark as life got, God was there to navigate me through the journey. And not just me, but each person in my new blended family. No, it is not always sunny and warm, it still rains - but it feels more like liquid sunshine; especially when I see the rainbow.

Finally, trusting that God has the power to transform our beautifully broken lives is where we find strength. Peace is part of our inheritance from God that means we can freely receive it just because we belong to God's family. We can also freely pursue peace as we encounter chaos and suffering in the lives of others. Jesus reminded the disciples at a time when He knew they would mourn His death on the cross, to receive His peace and not to allow themselves to stay in fear (John 14:27).

There are so many restless people who are hurting all around us. What's so good about the grief is that on the other side of pain, there is meaningful life. God is stronger than our grief. I dare you to hope and choose to embrace the change that is happening in spite of the trauma. The next time you encounter a rainy day, don't let it keep you indoors. Your hurt would like to hold you hostage, but God's joy can give you the strength to go the distance. There is goodness even when we grieve, there is comfort when we mourn, beauty for our ashes and healing for our wounds. On the other side of loss and grief, there is life and hope. We remain beautifully broken because He can heal us and show us that He is stronger than our struggle.

Hold on to hope, even when you have experienced grief and loss. When the unsuspecting ambush, fires down on you, your focus on hope will give you strength to survive. Jesus comes to be an anchor of hope so that when we drift, He has the power to keep us afloat. Getting honest with God and with yourself is a safe place to start. It's ok to wonder why, just as long you also meditate on how. Like the strength found in the grief warrior, Naomi, don't let your emotions keep you immobile. God desires to lift the cloak of heaviness that surrounds you.

Unpredictable twist and turns will enter each of our stories, but we must keep on fighting. The pain may feel like it is sneering at you with disdain, leaving you fragile and shaken; but we must use our weapons to fire back. In the struggle of grief and loss, remember the hope of heaven is stronger than your despair on earth. When an uncontrollable sensation surprisingly rises, it is ok to ride that wave with caution, just as long as you don't drown at sea. Hold on to the anchor and not to your unsteady emotions and circumstances. Beyond this dreadful season there will come a day when your throbbing soul will mend. This doesn't mean you are insensitive and have moved on with sorrow. It is an indication that the journey is rigorous and we must allow love to fuel our hearts and propel us onward.

God's comfort is stronger than your burdens. He picks up the pieces and shapes us into resilient people. He heals what is broken and develops us to grow stronger. Our experience in the warfare has not gone in vain, it has trained us. In this moment you realize your broken life has become a thankful one. Death has awakened you, and God has transformed you. Your mission is greater than your pain. Our hope does not disappoint, we remain committed to helping the living when they are injured and wounded. We show up in combat, aware of our scars and God's healing. She is a strong warrior who is insistent on holding on to the hope of eternity. She knows there will come a time when sorrow will cease and we will have won the war.

Strategic Battle Plans:

- Fight for life and hope
- Get honest with yourself and God
- Give yourself permission to trust
- Receive comfort from others
- Observe your scars as potential healing
- Embrace new growth
- Hold on to the hope of heaven

Declarations:

"The hope of heaven is stronger than my despair on earth."
"God's healing is greater than my hurts."

Hope is stronger than despair. Have you walked through a painful season of loss and discovered, like Naomi, all is not lost!

1. Unexpected change visits the life of Naomi. She gives herself permission to get honest by expressing to God her brokenness and bitterness after the loss of her loved ones. She chose to respond to her grief by going back to Judah and making room for God's presence. In her moment of despair, she allows comfort to come through her daughter-in-law, Ruth. Naomi receives hope to continue on the road to recovery.

2. We can humbly receive God's goodness by trusting Him to show up in our time of trouble. As Naomi heals, she becomes instrumental in helping Ruth find a new life with Boaz. Her pain is not permanent, because her focus on survival is being a blessing in the lives of others. God's shalom (peace) is upon her as she enters a new season with Him.

3. God takes all the broken pieces and creates a mosaic with a life that is willing to bring Him glory. Her life looked different, as she got through her time of despair and came to a place of hope. When we embrace God through every season, we can learn to live with no regrets. Our hurt would like to hold us hostage, but God's joy gives us the strength to go the distance. The author of life continues to write Himself into our story.

Notes and Scripture References:

How did Naomi's process of grief and loss help you deal with the challenges you are facing?

_____

_____

_____

_____

_____

_____

_____

_____

_____

_____

_____

Observations: A Joyful Life

o   Note the difference between being happy and living joyfully:

_____

_____

_____

_____

_____

_____

o Give yourself permission to get honest with God. What is something you find yourself struggling with?

_____

_____

_____

_____

_____

_____

o Embrace a new place. What is something you are believing God for?

_____

_____

_____

_____

_____

_____

_____

_____

_____

_____

Table Talk:

1. What is something you observed from the life of Naomi or Ruth that applies to you?
2. Have you ever walked through a desolate place in your heart? (Give yourself permission to get honest and talk about it.)
3. Tell about a time that someone showed you an act of kindness and it blessed you.
4. God calls us out of our comfort zone to trust Him, what is something you find yourself trusting God with?
5. Share about a time that joy was restored in your life.
6. In what ways can you become a blessing in someone else's life? Who are you going to bless, and how will you do it?
7. In what area of your life do you see God's hand at work?
8. What new beginning do you desire for God to bring into your life?

Application:

Bad things can happen to any one of us, but how we respond to these things changes our outcome. How do you respond to the challenge(s) you face in this season?

_____

_____

_____

_____

Home Project:

Count your Blessings:

Take a sheet of paper or journal and write out the many blessings you see active in your life.

My Prayer:

- This week I am praising God for:

- This week I am praying and believing God for:

- This week I pray to bless someone by:

Quality Time – Growing Stronger

Day 1: Read Romans 5:13
Today I want to receive hope and peace in this specific area of my life.

_____

_____

_____

_____

Day 2: Read Isaiah 55:10
Declare God's Word over someone in your life: state their name and speak God's promise.

_____

_____

_____

_____

Day 3: Read I Timothy 6:17-19
What good deed can I actively do in the life of someone else?

_____

_____

_____

_____

Day 4: Read Isaiah 61:4

Ask God to take the pain of what happened and begin to build something new in its place.

_____

_____

_____

_____

Day 5: Read James 1:2-8

Considering it ALL joy, what are some things God is working out for you?

_____

_____

_____

_____

Life Lesson 3

Battle with Anxiety ~ Wild and Free

"Something very beautiful happens to people when their world has fallen apart: a humility, a nobility, a higher intelligence emerges at just the point when our knees hit the floor."
- Marianne Williamson

Plunging in the pool with my nine-month old baby boy for lessons was my way of ensuring he would become a strong swimmer. Israel was already jumping off of a diving board into an Olympic sized pool by the age of four. My children love playing in the water with me. As a young girl, my family spent many summers at the water's edge and depending on how warm the water was, I would venture out into the deep. As I watched my siblings splash in the shallow end of the lake, I continued step by step, inching towards the deep. I drifted away from my family until I found myself kicking, panicking, and gasping for air. I lost my footing and was in over my head, unsure if anyone was watching. There are these unpredictable moments in life when our feet give way and we slip under the pressure, we drop from the load of stress. The sooner people notice, the safer our lives seem. Exhausted from it all, I sank further down like a heavy weight to the bottom. Suddenly there came a forceful grip that reached in and pulled me up by my bathing suit, into mid-air. Surely, in my shock I could hardly speak, I'm not even sure I said thank you. He was strong enough to carry my shivering frame, and he safely placed me on the sandy shore again, returning me to my family who seemed unaware.

Negative thoughts can pull you down like gravity, further into the deep. As you walk through the ups and downs of life, there are times we stumble and fall because our lives are out of balance. Overwhelmed by the weight, we wonder if anyone takes notice of us plummeting deep into the abyss. Miss Mary found herself needing unusual strength as she wrestled with the voices of seven demons. It was a tug of war for her soul as she battled toxic thoughts. It is disheartening when anxiety attacks and we cannot pursue relief or make practical decisions because we are full of worry. If only a mighty hand would come and pull us out from the darkness. Mary needed the hand of God to set her in a peaceful place, so she could stand.

Around the world and throughout generations, women must be ready to fight the cultural oppression that pushes them down or throws them off track. The warfare we encounter in life can trick us into thinking that our future is bleak. Anxiety strips us from obtaining what our heart values most, which is experiencing love, peace, and joy. How do we stop feeding the constant chatterbox of negativity? Mary soon discovered that real freedom was not beyond her personal reach. As with all of us, there are times that the answer to our dilemma is closer than we can imagine. She heard Jesus speak and it brought inner peace to her soul. Faith comes when you hear and believe God in your impossible circumstance. God doesn't overlook the confusion; He comes to the deep and picks you up.

The twelve disciples saw Jesus walking on the water while they were steering through a storm. It was Peter who called out to Jesus and decided to be with Him, even in the raging storm. He could have possibly drowned, but Peter was willing to be near Him even if it was dangerous. Jesus never criticized Peter for coming out to Him, instead He extends mercy and becomes the safety he needed. Jesus will be there in the middle of the storm to help you. Peter's faith was not reliant on his ability to walk on water, but his faith was contingent on trusting God's faithfulness, should he stumble. His faith moved him closer to Jesus even when he was afraid.

Experiencing God for the first time was a moment my heart will never forget. My mother called me and my four sisters to line up in the kitchen and hear the unbelievable news that my earthly father had passed away. She gently reminded us of the good news as well as the bad news, "Unfortunately your father will never hear how much you will miss him, but we are thankful he's been found." As a dazed twelve-year-old girl whose world had been totally shaken, I desperately wept, wanting my father to hear my request. My anger was consumed in my sadness and I was feeling anxious. So many thoughts tried to tear me apart, and yet somehow, I still knew my Heavenly Father was qualified to quiet my noise and comfort me in the shadow of my dad's death. His tenderness was near, and He spoke such peaceful words which steadied my heart. So, I leaned in and discovered that God was sheltering me from all the inner commotion that kept me in turmoil. He spoke into my heart by reminding me that He sees me and will continue to guide me. A peace that surpassed my understanding swept into my soul and faith broke through; bringing me to safety.

Until we receive the good news of Jesus Christ, we are hopelessly juggling a balancing act on a tight rope wondering if there is a net underneath to catch us should we fall. Often people are overwhelmed, under attack, and stressed out, finding themselves at a crossroad between circumstantial confusion and personal commitment. Tripping and falling is bound to happen, and like Mary, we must learn to fall forward on our knees and into His grace. Mary watches her Lord crucified and taking His final breath. She courageously marched towards the empty tomb of a resurrected Savior. For the rest of her days, she never loses sight of the one who saved her soul and filled her spirit with resurrection power.

There are times when fear and anxiety attack, but the Lord fights for you. The power of Christ is stronger than your anxious thoughts or disappointing setbacks. Mary received freedom when she allowed the words of Christ to override the words of the enemy. The light of Jesus pushes out the darkness, and illuminates the path that clearly leads to peace. Mary never stops listening to His voice and always keeps walking, a disciple of Christ for the rest of her life.

God knows when you are discouraged, tired or frustrated.

He also knows we struggle. He is stronger than anything you are going through. We can be free to embrace the abounding life we were created for. His truth will show you the way out by showing you the way that leads to Him. He is there in the deep to lift us out and set our lives in the right direction.

Some struggles we fight aren't as visible to the world, because these battles reside deep within our soul. The target is covered and the danger appears invisible. Although you feel marked, people aren't quick to catch that you've been on the frontlines for quite some time. When you are overlooked, you genuinely wonder if anyone cares. Who has your back? Who will jump in? You may find yourself wondering if God even cares? Feeling frail, depressed, and anxious are raging storms that swell if not dealt with properly. God does pay attention to all of the tension making its home in you. He is ready to take action on your behalf.

If God watches over the lilies in the vast fields and gently clothes each fragile flower, then imagine how much more He delights in wrapping you with His peace? When elements attack you, He speaks peace in the middle of your chaos. He is alert and sees what is happening. Under His attentive care, He reaches for the hurting sparrow that falls from the tree. God brings strength where it is needed because He upholds everything.

In your anxious struggle, you will discover that God's compassion is more powerful than your chaos. Like the freedom warrior, Mary Magdalene, she experienced the prince of peace clear out her past and present confusion. Leaving behind the darkness of depression, she resolves to let God illuminate her way. The path is peace. You will not be abandoned on the sidelines because, He sees you and moves with compassion to free you. His hand reaches for you and transcends a peace that surpasses all your understanding. His freedom is stronger than your fear. He provides a plan and a path that leads you to wholeness. God is at war and will crush your enemy and free you from his grip. The devil steals and destroys, but it is God's goodness and mercy that comes when you follow. You have not been left defenseless and vulnerable; He will give you courage as you rest in His faithfulness. When life feels fragile, remember the gentle lily that remains in the soil. When circumstances prevent you from flying as wild and free as the sparrow, remember His concern for you can lift you. When the storm is raging and the elements are taking over, He speaks peace and order.

You must fight to pursue peace because it will lead you to abundance. She is strong because she finds strength in the one that cares for her soul. God's peace will not allow you to fall apart when the world around you seemingly is.

Strategic Battle Plans:

- Take every thought captive to the knowledge of Christ
- Become mindful of your thoughts and words
- Submit to the authority of Christ
- Redirect fear and worry, refusing to let it stay
- Pursue God's peace

Declarations:

"God's freedom is stronger than fear's grip."

"Peace can transform my chaos."

God's freedom is stronger than your struggle with depression. As a disciple of Jesus, we have been given the ability to live with resurrection power just like Mary Magdalene.

1. Our mind is a battleground where God's truth triumphs over the attacks of anxiety. God takes captive every evil thought and delivers us from bondage. There is an invitation for all people to come to the cross of Christ and leave behind the influences we formerly followed.

2. We are invited to listen and obey God's voice as His truth confronts the battle that rages in our mind. The truth liberates us from the opinions of others and from having to please people at the cost of pleasing the one who can bring ultimate freedom to our soul. A disciple is one who willingly submits to the authority of the scriptures.

3. The Great Commission empowers us to share the good news that encourages, strengthens and comforts. The Holy Spirit walks with us as and equips us for victory in the days ahead. We have been called to reach others with the power of the good news.

Notes and Scripture References:

How does Mary Magdalene overcome her depression? What has the life of Mary taught you? (found in the four Gospels) Present at the crucifixion, Matt. 27:56; Mark 15:40; John 19:25; at the sepulcher, Matt. 27:61; 28:1–7; Mark 15:47; 16:1–7; Luke 23:55, 56; 24:1–7; John 20:1, 11–13

_____

_____

_____

_____

_____

_____

_____

_____

_____

_____

_____

Observations: A Life of Freedom

o   How did your life change once you chose to follow Christ? Note the difference between hearing the truth and knowing the truth:

_____

_____

_____

_____

Getting OVER: Write down how you feel and what God promises.

Overworked: REST:

Overlooked: VALUED:

Overwhelmed   PEACE:

Table Talk:

1. What is something you observed from the story of Mary Magdalene?
2. Share about the time you surrendered your heart to Christ. What changed about your life?
3. The Angel "rolled the stone away", share a time when you saw God do something supernatural.
4. Tell of an event when you experienced God through other people. What did they do for you?
5. Share a time you felt God prompting you to be a witness so that someone could learn about Jesus. What happened?
6. Tell us about a moment when you experienced God's freedom. How did your life change?
7. Now that you are living as a disciple of Jesus, share a way you are able to go and tell others through what you do.

Application: What would Jesus do?

As a disciple for Christ, pick one character trait you would like to have that reflects Christ.

My Prayer:

What is the Holy Spirit saying to me?

- To be still and know that He is God: (Psalm 46:10)
- For peace to guard over my heart and mind (Philippians 4:7)
- To come and find rest for my weary soul: (Matthew 11:28)

Write your testimony: (elevator version, three minutes)

_____

_____

_____

_____

_____

_____

_____

_____

_____

_____

_____

Quality Time – Growing Stronger

Day 1: Read John 6:31
Memorize something the bible says is true about God. How does that liberate you?

_____

_____

_____

_____

Day 2: Read John 10:3-5
Ask God to help you listen to His voice. What are you hearing God say?

_____

_____

_____

_____

Day 3: Read Luke 24:5,6
Seeking the living among the dead, what is something God is asking you to walk away from?

_____

_____

_____

_____

Day 4: Read 2 Corinthians 3:17
Share an area that you want to see God bring freedom.

_____

_____

_____

_____

Day 5: Read Philippians 4:8
Write this verse down, then pick one of the adjectives. Be intentional to think and write down what comes to mind:

_____

_____

_____

_____

Life Lesson 4

Battle with Significance ~ A Hidden Treasure

"We must go further. Beyond evaluating our current life experience and becoming clear as to whether or not our days' efforts are meaningful to us, we must set a new and more proactive course for our lives." – Brendon Burchard

I remember, as a young child playing the game hide and go seek. On Saturday afternoons the neighborhood friends would gather and play in the backyard. Someone begins to count, and quickly they all scatter. The goal is to find an excellent spot to tuck away and quietly stay, unseen till early evening. Long after the game was over, my friend Sam would remain all to herself in that small, remote hiding spot. We finally gave up looking for her, hoping she knew it was time to go home. I wondered how long before my little friend realized she didn't have to hide anymore.

Have you ever desperately searched for something and just gave up in the process? I have lost my keys, my phone, my glasses, I have even lost my way. In those moments, I am normally hunting and searching for clues that would guide me. For adults, hiding is something you can really get good at. There are plenty of untold issues and wrong decisions that are upsetting or embarrassing and better left unseen. The danger is that many things can grow in the dark and leave us imprisoned to bigger things like fear, rejection, guilt, and shame. The clutter grows in our closets and the confusion keeps growing in our hearts, eventually it leaves us searching to find the right path.

The thirsty Samaritan woman would leave her home, undetected, fetching her empty pots to fill at the well. She strategically left at a time when others weren't around, perhaps to avoid the neighborhood gossip and the condescending looks of the people in her community. Life was complicated having endured several divorces and a colorful past that trailed behind her. She longed to feel valued and significant, but remained hidden in her sadness. Walking through the desert in the heat of the day, was a reflection of the dry and desolate places in her fragile heart.

No matter where she went, people talked about her background like a bestselling novel. In the heat of the day, Jesus, the savior of the world, was waiting to show her something that no one else could. She had yet to experience healthy relationships that did not leave her broken and hurt. The people in her life were always on the take, especially the people who were a part of her jaded past. Wandering aimlessly, year after year left her going in circles without any evidence that it would get better. Jesus was ready to take her beyond her shame and help her discover her beautiful purpose. He shows up in our hiding spots to reveal the truth about who He is and to show us a better way to live.

Fear will paralyze the possibilities of what God can do for you. Fear will imagine what is not true and hold you hostage in falsehood. We doubt that people are unable to handle the authentic side of us. We may think that if people knew how short fused we are, they may not like us. We see them as wavering skeptics, and prefer to remain acquaintances rather than close friends. The fear of not being accepted causes us to disconnect and veil our wounded hearts. We refuse to have deep and meaningful relationships that rely on being transparent and truthful about our journey.

The real me felt isolated and unimportant, my married friends invited me to join them on outings, but because I no longer had a significant other, I made excuses to opt out. My desperate situation, left me living as a victim of isolation. As a single mom with two growing little ones at home, I struggled with insecurity. I felt like my problems were inconvenient for others so I buried parts of my story that could possibly make other people feel burdened. I didn't want people to feel like they had to walk on pins and needles taking care of me. I was uncomfortable with the whispers people shared amongst themselves because of me. I wanted to wait until I had it all together before I joined their circles.

Truth confronts our excuses and blatantly exposes our secrets. Jesus reveals to the woman at the well that He is the Messiah and the gift of God that wants to be generous in her life, not someday when she gets it all together, but right now in the middle of the struggle. He lets her know that God is greater than her cultural background, as well as her painful history. Seeing her rejection, Jesus is ready to quench the thirst in her soul as she is willing to become honest and transparent. He continues to get past the surface, until she reaches the spring of pure clean water. It begins to spill out, when she discovers something beautiful that flows from the inside of her.

Periodically, my husband Larry gathers our children and unpacks his growing up years and the lessons he's learned on the farm from early morning chores, caring for the animals, and living in a very large household. We found out first hand on a seventeen-hour family road trip to visit his humble beginnings in Midwest North Dakota. The farm represented lots of honest, hard work that was built on the principle of sowing and reaping. He attributes much of what he learned on the farm to becoming a purposeful business man. Larry values something even more than the life lessons on the farm. He values the moment Jesus came into his heart and gave him a new purpose for living. He continues to make it his business to demonstrate serving others as a priority. We are still reaping from the harvest that was cultivated in the earlier years of Larry's life. My little treasures have yet to realize all the hidden possibilities in each of their hearts and how God wants to use them.

God does not tolerate the excuses that keep us blocked from potential. His plan and our purpose are greater than we know. He expects for us, like this woman at the well, to give Him our empty pots so He can refill our hearts with living water. His purpose will expand far greater than you thought possible. It is not about self-survival, but something larger that encompasses others. He made you to know that you are appreciated by God and significant to His plan on the earth.

A few weeks ago, I was on a school mission trip with two of my high school daughters, Olivia and Trinity. It was there that I encountered this eleven-year-old girl. She was one of many children I would speak to that week, but her words still ring in my heart. She showed up that evening and found herself sharing how a few days ago she was missing. Her older sister's ex-boyfriend had taken her and a friend, late in the evening, to another city. She felt scared and heartbroken waiting in that apartment. On the second day, her dad came through the doors and rescued her and her friend out of that frightening situation. Wondering how she felt when she saw her dad, she finally looked up at me and sighed. She just knew for certain that he would not stop searching for her until she was found. With great relief she was soon back with her family and attending school again. She is receiving counsel, but she is genuinely thankful that her dad came through for her. It also made her think that she was alive for a reason. I frequently find myself praying for my sweet friend and God's beautiful plan in her life.

Jesus provides a way out of the wilderness and into His perfect, pleasing will. The woman at the well realized that she would never thirst again, not because she would never need water, but because she knew the source of her strength is found in coming to meet Jesus. His grace is stronger than your guilt, and your purpose is greater than your insecurities. What are you waiting for? The reason Jesus shows up, is to show you that your Heavenly Father has a precious plan for your life. He wants to pour out His love on you and through you so others can reach heaven with you. Our response is to simply say "Yes" and let Him in, then let Him use who we are. Our mission is to do everything for Him with all of our heart, mind, and strength for God's glory! *"Whatever you do, work at it with all your heart, as working for the Lord, not for human masters, since you know that you will receive an inheritance from the Lord as a reward. It is the Lord Christ you are serving."* (Colossians 3:23)

It's time to get honest, let truth invade your heart and allow Him to lead you out of the small hidden places you may be living. Jesus has the power to open the windows of heaven that bring in His glory and shut the doors to the way we did life outside of His will. He has the strength to keep you moving beyond your potential so you can discover the treasure that is hidden inside of you and live a life that honors Him.

How do we get ourselves in these small spaces? Have you ever put your hand in a glass jar and then realized although it's in there, you can't get it out? Do you break the glass jar and risk further injury? Do you just live with a jar on your arm, forever? There has to be something more, but what? Maybe it will come to you, but as you're waiting, you find yourself thinking about how useless your hand has become. Much like the useless hand, life has a way of seeming unimportant and insignificant.

As a soldier at war, you're fighting to overcome. The victory feels further than imagined. You decide to step back and settle in for a loss. Winning is far too difficult and the progress seems far too slow. Disillusionment has kept you removed and you are surrounded by this repetitive cycle that leaves you in defeat. The enemy shouts, "What's the use?" You agree, so you don't set any personal goals and you live with small agendas. Purpose and meaning are only to be desired, but never to be obtained. In reality, you place that all aside, finding yourself passive and settling for much less than you bargained for.

I believe so many of us are like the strong Samaritan woman at the well who was waiting for a breakthrough. She was quite the warrior, but she didn't realize it until Jesus showed up at the well. Like the hand stuck in the jar, women warriors feel trapped and forced to adapt. We are fighting to protect our hearts, but remain victims of our circumstances. You shake the undeniable betrayal, the harmful gossip, and the painful isolation only to discover that rejection continues to mark you, and insignificance keeps you as its victim. You find yourself fighting against the odds. Yes, you have been taken advantage of countless times and you would rather live removed, than suffer any further injury.

When we realize this battle is not just about our story, our experience, or our challenges, then maybe we would surrender to the notion that our lives are meant to be lived in a greater sphere. Far too often we allow our self-preservation to keep us small. We make such a big deal about how people are treating us, that we begin to hold back and we are afraid to take risks. The fiery darts come at you; life seems pointless, just a repetition of the day before. We shoot back because we respond to a personal attack, not to the mission on our lives. It seems that our agenda is always sabotaged by our family, our boss, and even our friends. We are serving the dreams and passions of other people who are pursuing their purpose.

Remember, you are a warrior who is determined to live for something more, like God's greatness. The problem with rejection is that you spend more time concerned about your sadness, than you do about making a difference. The kingdom of God has made room for you to step up and take position, to live with purpose and magnitude. Your life is best lived in unity with Christ and in serving your community. My life gets large when I think more about God's agenda for my daily life. As God calls you, He will equip you. She is strong because she finds greatness in reaching and serving others around her. She is not passive or wandering aimlessly. She moves forward by making decisions that determine God's purposeful direction in her life.

Strategic Battle Plans:

- Refuse to remain in small places that only make room for you
- Be present and responsive to God's plan
- Don't remain a victim of rejection
- Discover your purpose by seeing to the needs of others

Declarations:

"God's direction is stronger than my good intentions."
"A meaningful life makes a difference in the lives of others."

God's purpose is stronger than your struggle.

1. Bearing God's image is the reality check of who you are and why you exist. Making room in your heart for God's Word will continue to protect you from the things that pull you away from your purpose. Our fixation on the problem can cause us not to recognize Christ when He shows up in our moment.

2. God invites you to rely on His faithful character to lead us in your daily decisions. Authentic relationships are dependent on our ability to respond with honesty, even when it's difficult to do so. The truth reveals that God is generous and can do more than you ever imagined. Ask God to satisfy your needs, He is able to do exceedingly more.

3. The real estate of your heart is God's intended place of worship. God's love grows as it is generously given to others. release what the Lord has given you into the lives of others. God's purpose is demonstrated through your love for people. He is waiting on women to rise up and live out their purpose.

Notes and Scripture References:

Why is Jesus waiting to for this woman to show up? What happens to her as a result of her honesty? (found in the gospel of John 4:4-42)

_____

_____

_____

_____

_____

_____

_____

_____

_____

Observations: A Life of Purpose

- Celebrate small beginnings, "little is much when God is in it". What is an area you need to dedicate quality time to?

_____

_____

_____

_____

_____

_____

_____

_____

Application: Read Isaiah 61:7

- Draw a picture of rejection, note a time when you experienced rejection in your life:

```
REJECTION:



```

- Draw or note a time when you felt restoration, how did God help restore you?

```
RESTORATION:



```

Psalm 119: 129-134

Surviving insignificance, what is God inviting you to see about Him?

God's big dreams start with small steps. First write down a

dream God has placed in your heart, then write down a few steps you can take in this season to see it come to pass (give yourself deadlines).

_____

_____

_____

_____

_____

_____

_____

_____

_____

_____

_____

_____

_____

_____

_____

_____

_____

_____

Table Talk:

1. What is something that stands out to you about the Samaritan Woman's story?
2. Have you ever given God something you felt insecure about? What is it?
3. Talk about God's purpose in your life. Is there something you are believing God for?
4. We are called to acts of kindness, how does being in community bless you?
5. We can all feel lonely at times, looking back is there a moment when you realized God's faithfulness?
6. Big dreams start with small steps, what goal have you set in place to honor God's plan?

My Prayer:

_____

_____

_____

_____

_____

_____

_____

_____

_____

_____

_____

_____

_____

_____

Quality Time – Growing Stronger

Day 1: Romans 8:14-16
God has accepted you fully and His love completes you. Take a moment to give Him your insecurities.

_____

_____

_____

_____

Day 2: Read Psalm119:15-18
Ask God to open your eyes to the miracles hidden in His Word. Write what comes to mind:

_____

_____

_____

_____

Day 3: Read over John 4:10, then read Ephesians 3:20
God is generously finding ways to bless your life, what are you believing for in faith?

_____

_____

_____

_____

Day 4: Read over John 4:24, then read Psalm 142. Take a moment to write down why you praise Him for being God.

_____

_____

_____

_____

Day 5: Read Psalm 146:8-10. Listen to a song that talks to you about God's goodness, then write God a thank you note:

_____

_____

_____

_____

Life Lesson 5

Battle with Grit ~ Living Strong

"Grit has two components: Passion and Perseverance."
– Angela Duckworth

One of my first hiking adventures in the Pacific Northwest consisted of water, protein bars, and lots of positive determination. The trail was considered intermediate and I started off with a bang. About 3/4 of the way in, I was breathing heavy walking up a steep ascent. I had to motivate myself with lots of self-talk and cheering, I honestly felt like both a rookie and a coach. Although I was mentally ready to give up, I refused to stop. I kept pressing and was soon rewarded by a fellow traveler on his return down from the summit. Seeing the sweat on my face, he smiled and said, "The hard part is over, not much further!" Then suddenly I was encouraged to dig a little deeper and mustered enough desire to keep on going. Yes, I encountered the remarkable summit and it was well worth the climb!

Stay the course with Christ, even when the road is long and arduous. Consistency over time is the key to a powerful life. Christ has already climbed your mountain and will faithfully guide you from start to finish (Philippians 1:7). He is able to strategically use your desires in calibration with your ability to push through your areas of great challenge. He has a plan for you to go the distance! God is effectively linking your glorious journey on earth to what will be your eternal journey in heaven. He raises a standard and holds us accountable so that we can decide to not settle for anything but His best. You will come to realize; it will be worth the climb.

On a trip to the Dominican Republic, where my parents were born, I took a few days to go visit my paternal grandfather. When I arrived at his doorsteps, my cousins welcomed me in as if I had always been a part of their lives; forever. After I hugged each neck, they stepped away and made room, for this small, frail, bright-eyed man who embraced me with the strength of a bear. As I caught my breath and landed back on my feet, my grandfather led me into the living room, telling me stories and showing me memorable pictures and achievements of my family. They were successful in both the marketplace and on the mission field, but my grandpa pointed upward letting me know that real success comes from being rooted in God. Our family tree has grown strong because of this. He then regrettably shared that my dad walked away from our family, including God's love.

My grandfather never gave up praying for us even though

we lived many miles away. I never knew that being in his home was an answer to his many years of passionate prayers. It was beyond heavenly to think that, before I could impress him with my dazzling personality, I was already accepted, loved, celebrated, and prayed for. He held my face tenderly and reminded me that God has not forgotten me, then kissed me on the forehead. His fervent prayer was one of the many reasons I was experiencing God in my everyday life. I was standing on the strength of others, so it was necessary for me to pick up my baton and keep running my personal race for Jesus. I couldn't help but think it was my turn to take responsibility for my calling, to persevere through prayer and to faithfully believe that my life could make a difference. It filled my heart knowing I am a small part of a godly heritage that is beautiful, growing, and strong.

The Apostle Paul would turn to his spiritual son, Timothy, and remind him to finish strong. It was Paul's highest priority to leave a lasting spiritual legacy for Christ that would outlive him and reach future generations. God wants to make a deposit on the earth through hearts that are willing to remain submitted to Him. Paul ran his race like others were depending on it. Knowing that his earthly departure was near, he hands the spiritual baton to Timothy. Entrusting him with the truth, he encourages Timothy to focus on fulfilling his earthly mission. This young leader is challenged to keep on fighting, keep on running, and keep on believing. Paul writes, "*I have fought the good fight, I have finished the course, I have kept the faith*" (2 Tim 4:7).

My strength training coach often chants words of encouragement as we are pushing through the threshold of resistance. As athletes, we must be tenacious. As warriors, we must engage in the battle. When opposition comes, you must position yourself beforehand to not give up. You must calculate your options, stop reacting, and start evaluating the opportunities you have to win. The power punch will always come from the place of God's purpose. You must allow Him to go with you, "...*ultimate victory comes from the Lord, God*" (Proverbs 21:31). The Lord is mighty in battle. He is defending you, while He is destroying the enemy. Even when your emotions want the final word, it's essential to submit to God's way of doing things. As you see His strategy, you discover that there is a clear distinction between what you must fight for and who you must fight against. Exercise your (passion) muscle because it may be the necessary action that will help you persevere until you see God's plan unfold. In a little while, you will be able to get through the difficulty knowing that the ultimate victory is on God's side.

God's way of winning will require humility, transparency, and love. Humility is hard to come by, first because it is unnatural to be humble. Without the work of the Holy Spirit, we will be at the center of our perspectives, desires, and dreams. I recall a heated conversation where I was relentlessly trying to convince my friend that I was doing the right thing. Unfortunately, not knowing when to stop, pull back, or walk away is dangerous. I came away winning an argument, but losing a friendship. Trust God with the ability to bring grace and transformation in His perfect time frame, not yours. We must be rooted in the love of Christ, not in our self-righteousness as we interact with others. If God has the whole world in His strong hands, then why not hold on to Him instead of your opinions and sometimes small agendas?

You are hardwired for love and everything you do should be an expression of that. God's love will not turn you away or just give you what you want. He gives us the ability to give strength to others by creating an atmosphere that allows people to safely exhale, without the pressure of having it all together. It is important to have listening ears and become dependable partners in prayer. Love patiently steps into the messy parts of life and believes with you. Even in the conflict, love is longsuffering, it provides hope in the darkness. Love rescues you and puts you in the spot where faith can propel you. Love is the greatest gift you can possibly receive or give. It is essential to the human soul, and without it, we are capable of great evils. God's love generously redeems all who choose to come to Him. Love is the strongest force there is and will cause you to flourish, even when you are weak in the struggle.

It's time for you to grow stronger, being firmly planted in His word and rooted in His love. The magnificent roots found in the bamboo plant are the underlying force that help it to grow tall. These tall grassy plants remain underground and at surface level they don't appear to be growing, but they are committed to continuous growth as they shoot up quickly, growing at a rapid rate, visible to the natural eye. Their growth may even appear unstoppable. There are a variety of ways in which this tall, strong plant proves to be useful. We may have meager beginnings and appear weak in light of our humble circumstances, but for all who are rooted in Christ, you have been given something that will produce continuous growth. There is an underlying force that will spring up and allow us to get taller and stronger than ever. You can rise up from the ashes because deep within you is something that is cultivated in the heart. It will spring up to become visible and strong enough to inspire others as you continue to live out your earthly mission.

God's goal is to move you forward and upward, so keep on believing in the one who can be strong for you. The enemy of your soul desires to defeat you and keep you from God's ultimate best in your life. When you are tired and vulnerable, your heart must guard against the relentless bouts of disappointment, discouragement, and disillusionment. Allow your soul to receive water and rest as you stay close to God's presence. Activate your faith and trust God's leading because He has great plans for your meaningful life.

The equation is quite simple, if I ask for God's wisdom and add it to my situation, it can still produce something glorious. Whenever I am at a deficit, there is still no cause for alarm because even my trials have the ability to turn up for something good. The active living word, that stood the test of time, will never pass away because it has the transforming power to change the way we think and act today. You are never left to figure things out on your own because you have access to the faithful loving God. The reason we can be inspired through the testimonies of others, is because God is the common denominator in each of these comeback stories.

He is intricately involved in your design and in your destiny. Our God can meet each of your needs from His eternal storehouse and we must turn to Him. These principles are timeless, so let them impact you in such a way that you are never without hope. He desires to equip and empower you in Christ. Your life is best lived for His glory, so my sister, carry-on in the strength of the Lord and remember, YOU are strong!

"Quotes"

"When one has fully entered the realm of love, the world, no matter how imperfect – becomes rich and beautiful, it consists solely on opportunities to love."
Kierkegaard, Søren. Works of Love. Princeton University Press, 1847.

"All the adversity I've had in my life, all my troubles and obstacles have strengthened me." - Walt Disney

"Something very beautiful happens to people when their world has fallen apart: a humility, a nobility, a higher intelligence emerges at just the point when our knees hit the floor." - Marianne Williamson

"We must go further. Beyond evaluating our current life experience and becoming clear as to whether or not our days' efforts are meaningful to us, we must set a new and more proactive course for our lives".
Burchard, Brendon. The Motivation Manifesto 9 Declarations to Claim Your Personal Power. Hayhouse, 2014.

"Grit has two components: Passion and Perseverance."
Duckworth, Angela. GRIT The Power of Passion and Perseverance. Scribner, 2016.

Author

Eileen Hunter Wolf

With a background in communication and leadership, Eileen is easy to understand and encouraging to talk with. She has served in full-time ministry for twenty-five years, teaches the word at her local church, and travels speaking in venues around the world. Eileen is the founder of an online platform called We Grow Stronger, a tool used to help all people develop their faith in Christ.

People describe her as energetic and inspirational. She helps you understand and find practical truth that will strengthen you on your life's mission. Eileen currently resides outside of Seattle with her husband, Larry and their four children: Lauren, Olivia, Trinity, and Israel. She is also a proud owner of two pampered dogs, Winston and Wesley.

Eileen is always thrilled to hear from her readers. Subscribe and connect with her on www.wegrowstronger.org and on social media @eileenhunterwolf.

CPSIA information can be obtained
at www.ICGtesting.com
Printed in the USA
FSHW011451070619

9 781937 400538